TWELVE CLAY TABLETS

TWELVE CLAY TABLETS

*A Structural History of Mesopotamia
in Twelve Poems*

by J. A. Gucci

Pressure System Press
New York, New York

2026

Published by Pressure System Press

First edition

ISBN: 978-1-972788-00-4

Printed in the United States

Teaching materials and extensions:
www.jagucci.com

CONTENTS

How to Use This Book

Each page contains a short poem. You are not being asked to interpret it in the usual way. Instead, focus on what is happening.

Look for:

- what condition is present
- what changes
- what remains consistent over time

Each poem corresponds to a system from ancient Mesopotamia.

As you read, try to identify how the system works. The goal is not to explain the poem, but to recognize the pattern.

As you move through the book, notice how these patterns repeat and sustain a stable civilization.

The tablet of the gods is written in clay.
— Mesopotamian proverb

Weir

Braided
shallow streams,
milky
shifting gravel bars—
crumbling bank.

Water-logged
logs in a stream bed,
vertical stakes
wedged in mud—

rock bowl.

Waggle Dance

Waggle dance—
dust
scraped onto legs,

saddlebags—
stuffed
inside a cell.

Fermenting hexagons
sealed with wax—

bee bread—
royal jelly.

Seal

Wet grey
river mud
scooped—
kneaded,

press—lift
press—
downstroke—

raised lion.

Floodplain

Crushed mountains
surging over bank—
slumped black
seeping mud.

Eel grass
splayed on canyon walls,
sun-bleached pillars—
iron red—

mud polygons.

The Great Migration

Solar noon—
petrichor.

Sunk flanks—
eyes,
emaciated ribs.

Blue wildebeest
piling—

leap—
jaw-snap.

Mass Spawning

Clownfish in a crevice,
eel in a crack—
limestone labyrinth.

Marine snow—
drifting pink
eggs—

 neap tide.

Mollisol

Yellow
dangling from spikes,
white
silky stem hair—

turkey foot—
cementing silt,
clay—

black mollisol—
sod house.

Forest Edge

Sideways sunlight,
compressed winds—
thickets.

Whirling—
dry,
cool,
damp heat—

vigilance.

Allelopathy

Slow growing
succulent—
swollen with water,

burrows under shrubs,
cool umbra under
ironwood.

Cracked seed—
ring of sand—
leaching,
seeping—

tangleweed.

Levy

Wet seeds
splayed under sun,
dry in the chamber.

Harvesters clip a sprout—
rotting husks—
sweet black
crumbled soil—

seething.

Dry Basin

Jagged grey
cracked dirt—
dust.

Bear in a bin—
broken bird feeder—

rotting hollow
hive.

Burn Scar

Blazing—
plumes of black
turpentine air.

White ash
horizon—
alight on log,
charred—

fireweed.

APPENDIX

These poems present historical development through observable systems.

Each entry corresponds to a condition within early Mesopotamia—formation, storage, boundary, migration, surplus, depletion. The systems shown are not symbolic substitutions. They are structural parallels. A change in the physical system reflects a change in the historical one.

Each poem operates through three elements:

- A condition that holds
- A threshold where change occurs
- A resulting state

This triadic structure organizes transformation without explanation.

Example:

Weir

Water is slowed, redirected, and contained. Flow crosses a boundary and becomes storage. The system shifts from movement to control.

The same structure appears historically in early irrigation practices, where rivers were shaped into channels and basins to support settlement.

The poem does not describe this directly. It presents the structure.

Reading

Approach each entry by identifying:

- What condition is present at the start
- Where the threshold occurs
- What state remains after the change

Meaning emerges from the relation between these elements.

The sequence of poems traces a progression:

Formation → Organization → Storage → Expansion → Stress → Depletion → Renewal

The systems change. The structure remains.

The Twelve Series

Each book in this series presents systems through short, structured poems.

Rather than describing events, the poems model how systems form, interact, and change over time.

Each volume focuses on a different civilization, using the same method to reveal how complex societies develop.

History

Mesopotamia — Formation
Greece — Interaction
Rome — Expansion and Collapse
Medieval — Thresholds

Creative Writing

Twelve Small Windows
Twelve Loops
Twelve Mirrors
Twelve Rooms

Philosophy

Twelve Iron Paradoxes

ABOUT THE AUTHOR

J. A. Gucci is an educator and writer whose work
focuses on systems, structure, and the relationship
between form and meaning.

His books present historical and conceptual
material through short, structured poems designed
to model how systems form and change over time.

COLOPHON

This book was set in a clear, readable typeface to
support careful observation and sustained
attention.

The poems follow a consistent structure to
emphasize pattern, repetition, and continuity over
time.

Designed and produced as part of the Twelve
series.

www.ingramcontent.com/pod-product-compliance
Lightning Source LLC
Chambersburg PA
CBHW021350060726

47591CB00006B/2243